Mirrorball

ALSO BY JOHN MUCKLE

It Is Now As It Was Then (with Ian Davidson)
The Cresta Run
Bikers (with Bill Griffiths)
Cyclomotors
Firewriting and Other Poems
London Brakes
My Pale Tulip
Falling Through

CRITICISM
Little White Bull: British Fiction in the 50s and 60s

John Muckle

Mirrorball

Shearsman Books

First published in the United Kingdom in 2018 by
Shearsman Books
50 Westons Hill Drive
Emersons Green
BRISTOL
BS16 7DF

Shearsman Books Ltd Registered Office
30–31 St. James Place, Mangotsfield, Bristol BS16 9JB
(this address not for correspondence)

www.shearsman.com

ISBN 978-1-84861-597-7

Copyright © John Muckle, 2018.

The right of John Muckle to be identified as the author of this work
has been asserted by him in accordance with the
Copyrights, Designs and Patents Act of 1988.
All rights reserved.

Acknowledgements
Thanks is due to the editors of *Angel Exhaust, Blart, Eyewear, Festschrift for Tony Frazer, Great Works, Intercapillary Space, Jacket, Molly Bloom, Pages, PN Review, Spine, Tears in the Fence, Tux Deluxe, The Warwick Review* – where some of these poems first appeared.

Contents

Nothing Wrong	9
Poetry and Philosophy	10
Ladder of Causes	11
Elizabeth Bishop	12
Poor Richard's Almanac	13
An Estuary	15
A Night at The Crown	17
Poem for Denise	18
Moving Around	21
Snuggling in an Old Man's Bed	23
Blue Square	25
Rear Window	26
Residues	27
The Old Unitarian Chapel, Taunton	28
I Should Be So Lucky	29
On Ebury Bridge Road	31
My Joy, My Reason, My Dwelling	33
Sleeping and Waking Up	34
The Fairy Castle	35
Journey to Edmonton	37
Looking Babies	39
In the Bright Room	41
These Stories	42
She Walks in Beauty	43
A Lily for My Love	45
Being Beauteous	46
A return of spirit	47
Against Cutting	48
Rainham Interchange	49
Nautical Miles	51
John and Joan Elliot	53
For Tom and Val	55
This Star Makes Us Want to Lie Down	57
Walking After Midnight	58
The Beacons	59
In the Still of the Night	61

Three Dragonflies	63
What Rough Draft	64
Wasley's Parrot	65
Being Bounteous	66
High Talk	67
Sonnet for Anne	69
To a Squirrel	70
Chew Tar	71
Greenwich Meridian	72
Dubious Parameters	76
Self-Portrait in a Compact	78
Cognitive Mapping	80
Life in a Bowl	82
Autumn's Schedule	83
Mirrorball	85

In memory of Pamela Mary Muckle (née Fenton)
February 1932 – May 2018

Nothing Wrong

Nothing went wrong, it was meant to be this way
curling around its dense privet hedges over
which you pretended not to see your future –
a lawn being mown, the click of edge trimmers,
a strimmer starting up like a yawning siren.

Those plans you made were the mislaid plans
of a mouse, striding out with an alert nose, a pert
mouse who was at any rate single-minded,
anything smelling of cheese being just the job
under the shadow of the winning-post-tree.

Nothing changed in all the years you knew her
turning up out of the blue like that, returning.
Her trail of footprints always ended at the border.
Only once did you catch her weaving, once or
twice a slip of the tongue made you wonder.

Nothing gone wrong, it was meant to be this way,
her payment in kind is for the right-wrong reason
and your heart is broken for a mess of pottage.
Babies crying for their fathers; in the evening
brilliant new stars will be coming out for them.

Poetry and Philosophy

Poetry is the poor man's philosophy
The lamp by which he finds solace
A light significant only for what he reads by it
A subject without agency
Tormented nevertheless by guilt
Poetry is the poor man's apology

Philosophy is a poor apology for poetry
Dry bandages on a fresh wound
Absorbent wrappings for all that is bloody
All comprehending and surpassing
Whispered beneath sepulchres
Philosophy is poetry's winding-sheet

Poetry springs out of the mouths of babes
Philosophy's sense is contested and cumulative
Poetry goes on about the landless peasantry
Philosophy believes the poor are superfluous
Poetry is convinced it has solutions
Philosophy admits its knowledge is worth nix

Believe that and you'll believe anything
Coming up against brick walls and singing round them
Echoes bouncing back, as clear as day
Into the eyes and ears and hearts of the poor
Philosophy is the rich man's poetry
It has put food on his table, brought him happiness

But what do you mean by poetry? Philosophy?
I mean clear singing of the heart's desires
A rigorous interrogation of the word
A knot of images and sounds and thoughts
And I mean to wind the world back onto its spool
So it will play out quickly if a fish grabs it

Ladder of Causes

The first you hear of them they're getting better
But before long you wake up under their rule.
One has stolen your woman, another is sliding by
In a greatcoat you had been thinking of wearing
Against the chill of prophesied ill-weather.

Whether to stay or go is a question that troubles you
Too late to ask in light of compulsory expulsions
As a dolphin leaps through its hoop, clucking
Like a red hen, smiling at its approaching brother
As their paths cross in mid-air, that's the truth.

I hear they have set up a commission of enquiry
Which announced remission of its further sins.
Omission, perdition, who can doubt their efficacy
When, after all, injustice requires no clear wins,
It's simply the outcome of fair competition?

Rumours of war is as good as winning ashes
To tunes of a tin can orchestra, a whistle blows down
Lava all over your stirrup; no way up in the world
You're in the saddle of a hoarse almighty laugh.
Your children were as good as theirs, you thought.

Ladder of causes, grid of lights, a mayfly moon.
Over the valley is a brighter day. I love my mother.
At the top of the town is the bottom line, and all
These bright young care-creatures, what are they thinking?
They are thinking of the good things in the sky.

Elizabeth Bishop

In Elizabeth Bishop's poem, 'Filling Station',
the mechanic and his greasy sons are saying,
Sure, we're greasy, that's what we do, lady,
we grease your car, and we are who we are,
God loves us; and my good wife, our mother
oils that plant you seem to admire so much
and she lays out those grey doilies on the table.
She thinks we're okay. Alice, tell the lady.

Thankfully it's thanksgiving, the four of them
are sitting down to a well-earned turkey dinner,
basted in recycled engine-oil, and on the hill
specklike children play with fire, an old wrench,
beneath the lowering echolalia of a sky, the terms
of whose sympathy are difficult to accept.

Alice puts down her sewing needle, it's carved
from a wishbone, she folds the pure white overalls
and sits at the table. No grace has yet been said.
She says none either, but her three sons thank her
quietly for their dinner before returning to their
abuse of a pig of a job, another ugly customer.

A headless chicken wanders in from the road,
asks if its poor life isn't worth just a bit more than
the poet woman's abrupt use of it as a splash of colour.
The mechanics aren't listening, as usual. Alice
rearranges their words into a song, praising her,
hissing sibilants tell you to shh, shh, shh, be quiet
about this scene, it's from a life not your own.

Poor Richard's Almanac

"Not to oversee workmen is to leave them your purse open."
   ——Benjamin Franklin

Open your mind to a scholar
And you pass your baby to grandma wolf
To mind while you stir the pot
Your mind aloof.

How many rungs in a ladder?
How many fish in the sky?
Eat one boiled fish for your supper.
Hold the string of your kite upon high.

Spend a penny on soda pop
That penny is one will please you not
By rubbing shoulders with another
Multiplying by the foot.

Conjugate your farthings!
Good grammar is cumulative
Additionally, may I say,
Drink water frugally, on tap: you'll live.

My mind is like a fine-meshed sieve
That sifts its gold from the silt;
Lets the dross pass right through it,
Puts tiny nuggets in its belt.

A man I know lent his fastest horse
To a fool running a fool's errand.
That fool was no such fool, he sold it
And ran on foot to Maryland.

O count your losses, slowly
Or count them quick, who cares?
Count them a hundred times, if you please:
But look well to your fiscal affairs!

When riding out to the slave markets
A boy told his plangent tale;
It appeared to amuse him greatly
How a wise man sold shit by the pail.

On such and such a day a ship arrives
In New York harbour, with a cargo of fresh coffee;
Offer your old stock at full price, half price,
A free cup advertises your honesty.

But they've stolen my sharpest of saws,
I put down my saw-book someplace.
A letter's an odd shape, a chicken untoothed,
A saw-horse? No stirrups, no grace.

I may frame my partial insights,
I may say what I wish night and day;
What I say will fall short of the highest truth,
My saws are flexed horses, in flight.

An Estuary

I like that part of the county, the way mist rises
off salt-marshes, a flat, humpy landscape of pylons
appearing to go on forever, circles back on itself

as if it were visible to the naked eye, the North sea
hiding concrete watchtowers, each one a great polis
which has stood off invading waves and the yachts

of the snaky Deben, scything deep channels in mud
on its banks picnics, wanderings with the dog
along a raised culvert that pulls you toward land

and the low bungalows, spaced like breakwaters
weathered havens, leaning rickety boathouses
assembled by centuries of tides, full of bad paintings

and dimple bottles hung in string bags at windows,
each winch crowned with its own barnacle knot.
Crabbing up a champion crab with nil equipment

then it's a swift pint or two of Adnams in the snug
a light or two bobbing, the land itself uncertain
on a weekend with kids, blotto under canvas,

lying back with that filtered light on your eyelids
cooking up a big feed of burgers on the sixties
camping stove, words trailing off, except to point,

exclaiming at a chain of starfish, a ribbon of kelp:
found jewellery requiring no skill, no patience
just a glow of happiness holding you for a moment

left behind with this year's other discoveries
maybe to push up out of the mud of memory sometime
soon, I hope, in the golden days of the future

of tributaries I got lost in, prising with the boat hook
happy enough in your sandals, your sailor suit
dripping with sweat, your forehead wide, untroubled

where your granddad used to live, under the sea,
and where I long to turn back I am joined to others
where it ends I don't know; in a deep, rough stitch.

A Night at The Crown

Already it was a hymn to the magic of retrospect,
a cathedral of nicotine, a country and western band
& denizens from the deeps of thirty-two counties
in family groups or, collars up, swimming dark tables
under dusty gold brocade, columns, ivory mouldings
held up by heavy grandfather clocks from the nineties.
The crack was mighty at the Crown; they played
MacAlpine's Fusiliers, Spancilhill, The Race Is On.

A heritage mural of day labourers awaiting hire
on the far wall – at least it was a job for a painter –
and twin low-slung leather settees, a Pole at the bar.
Upstairs, once a month: jazz, so it says on a poster.
I buy a pint and slip out to peek in through chained
doors of the back dance hall: alright, it's still there
as before, shrouded, stacked chairs, ready to burst
into life again, I hope, at some turn in the weather.

Once in Hammersmith I was accosted by an actor.
He was getting drunk at a table of friends. I'd popped
in on my way to the Irish Centre, perched a spare seat,
and he convinced me he was a relaxing Irish labourer
with a wink as broad as a slumming Brendan Behan.
I was just being polite, I thought, looking to get away,
when he revealed he was rehearsing for a future play.
In vague humiliation, I drank up and scuttled out.

I sit here, nurse my pint, wait for the action to start,
pull out my Nokia to compose a text message to you
telling you where I am right now, just guess, send it off
in its little winged envelope, make rings on the bar
symbolising those hoops through which I tried and
failed to jump. We talked, had a drink, moving back
to the vault, and listened to a kicking band playing
still in dark places I do not enter. *Céad Míle Fáilte.*

Poem for Denise

I wanted to say something
about Denise, my friend at work:
she is truly a beautiful person
but to insist on her, or
that, would be as unnecessary
as saying the winter will bring colder weather.
She will bring out her boots, and change into them
before going out in the snow
but never without finishing her chores,
because some things, anything important, really
can't be left to the children, not when you want it to be
done properly: you have to do it yourself, you have
to get down on your hands and knees, and into every corner,
then it's quite satisfying, in a way, to know
where everything is, when each speck
has been removed, and placed somewhere,
in a night-jar, handily beside her bed.

Her face is a brown moon, it is the setting off place
for a journey in praise of all things compact
and I know what I'm talking about.
The dark is her lover.
She isn't a plea bargainer, or a new way of making wars.
This isn't anything to do with love, and I'm not sure
what it is about, maybe it's just a way of saying
short people have their uses too as draft excluders.

Pretend you know everything about another's life, preach
equality and it will turn into its complete opposite.
Lying down in the middle of the gulf stream
isn't the same as putting your big toe on the hot tap
for another blast of heat. North is
just a direction, not a pole planted in the ground. Oh really?
I hear Denise saying a big nay, but she's only

telling the truth in her completely imperturbable way
and I am not lying to aver she is wiser than me
speaking of nothing much in a somewhat roundabout fashion
which I learned to do by copying another.
Who cares? Some jobs do your head in, and if you
Happen to be doing a job like that it's twice as hard.
There's usually one mean person in charge
and if that person doesn't like you, forget it, you might
as well give up and think about St. Kitts, or shopping
with interminable lists strapped to your money belt; expecting
the worst of such persons, you won't be disappointed
        but don't
change sides. Be aggrieved. If you are, you have no friends
but this is not a reason to get depressed (too much).
Next time get a job you like.

I know, strangely enough, how not to bother
about what others say they think of me, good or bad,
because what do they know, the fools?
This time everybody has been slightly more helpful
in response to my humble pleas for assistance.
Is the world ending
or am I just accidentally dying of something special?
In middle age we become heartily sick of these notions
which took so long to reveal themselves as false.
And some people always knew everything all along
so they'll say, if you can believe those liars
will turn out to have been actually telling the truth. It's not
something you want to think about anymore
not even dopily, for the benefit of a nearby brick wall.
The fiddler's thumbs twiddle with a piece of elastic.
The trombonist's slide has fallen off
due to that low note he couldn't resist trying out
for the benefit of Denise, or somebody else
he once knew, or once half-knew, or imagined; but it's not
her problem, or mine for that matter,
only a certain slant of sunlight that has betrayed you,

another tentacle to be lopped off by John Wayne's machete
during the octopus fight at the end of *The Wake of the Red Witch*
before his diving helmet filled up with sea-water
and he drowned, our bravest captain.

    Once, on Dagenham's dirty floors,
I thought of nothing but cleaning fluids, how often Flash
comes back to you as a desire for it all to sparkle, to say your prayers.
Germs, your days are numbered, all tagged lightning and the brightness
                                      of springs
While away endless days on hope: give up finally
in a sign of no despair. I know all this is untrue. And Denise
knows better. And I think it is quite frightening.
Wasn't I supposed to be cleverer? Aren't I still?
I pray for an answer,
I pray for a new cleansing power.
And nothing else will do anymore.

Moving Around

My first years back in London
were spent moving around
from high on the hill to the valley
where I had drunk with you

walking streets once known
now overgrown with writing
composed like greased lightning
but I never found you again.

I found the hard shoulder
instead, to cry on, a room with a torn
condom packet under a bed;
in a sock drawer I kept my dread.

On the way out of the station
a solemn little demonstration
of silent schoolchildren stepped
between guardian police cars.

Poor mites, they were in the gun wars.
I was in a pensionable job
where bullets were in the eyes
of the ladies who couldn't read or write.

Power-seeking missiles overhead
grazed at the skies of Iraq.
Some people blew up a tube train
and the top off a double-deck.

London stepped out to mourn.
We were deep underground
allowed only to keep silence
in that basement of cultural norms.

My plight was light, I floated
due North, into a nice little flat
between too many food outlets
and a place with the internet.

There's a quiet phone by my bed.
I am a quarantined survivor,
a bug in a rug. I am snug here
in a way, but I still know inside

there is nowhere much left to hide
only a place you can't forget,
your past unravelling like a dream
of mistakes you made in your life.

Snuggling in an Old Man's Bed

In Edinburgh the San Quentin prisoners did Endgame
Glasgow was a waltz across Texas,
At least a quick twirl around the station forecourt:
Happy to be there, under the blank eye of a forgotten statue
To win the cackling approval of some duffer
Que tu as aimé beaucoup, who greeted us, waltzing,
And Robert's edgy, red-headed scrawn was half-pacified.
We found a bar, she drank up a rum and black.
Ah wouldni mind a pitcher a hir. He'd drink up your last drop.
We drank up and caught a rattling suburban train
Out to the suburbs. Robert's grandfather's stop.

He was a delighted old man, when he set eyes on her,
Tiny, stooped, barely alive. Trouble wi' the waterworks.
We parked around his fire, a pale flicker in
The heat of late August; he demonstrated a shopping basket
Which pulled up his milk, lowered his moggie to earth.

Darkness falling, we listened as his memory
Tank refilled slowly. He'd seen service as a cavalryman
In the Russo-Turkish war; he was around our age,
Hadn't even the smallest clue what it meant.
Rob, amused, coaxed out another histoire familiale, a feud
He'd begun by letter with his older brother
A twenty-five year eye-blink earlier. But it wasnae
That, he said, I'd enough of him. I'd know soon enough.

We drank it all in, polished off a bottle of his malt
In vintage car tots. We were infanta and he would die
Soon in a room of musts, of creaking chairs, a tick far
Fainter than its tock; and then, at half-past-nine, it
Was time for our beds! Robert claimed the dusty couch.
The old cavalryman's eyes danced as he showed us
A back bedroom, a bolster on a sagging pin mattress.

Ye'll be warm enough, he said, a whistling reed
In his throat. Isabelle and me rolled together, wondering
If we'd stain the sheets. Wouldn't you know, we fell asleep.
In the morn those two great Scots eyed us jealously.

Blue Square

Let the smoke drift up to the blue sky
Eastertime, on Monday bank holiday
Feathers through a full glass of milk
O Daddy's little boy, my roly-poly,
How I'd like to have called you Roy.

French kisses, grammar, one two three
Leaves a silvered agony, it seems
Nought forming nought, equation's dream
The grime on a clean ceiling, a mirror,
Found artifacts from the daily dig.

Thumbprints on the door, and vinegar
To clean them with, a sheaf of songs
Will lull me to my rest beneath sods
On plotted ground intending crimes bought.
It doesn't pay to try so very hard.

Territories carved up between the alleged
A pink sparkly bag of incense sticks
Surmounted by an icon, chin in hand,
A white globe lantern dirtily lit up,
A candle for my hand, coffee, and pillows.

Twinkles for a tuning fork. I file a page.
My ink's as plentiful as North Sea gas
Steering for deep waters, away from the rage
That clicks in my synapses' rusty points
Riding high on a list of tacks, disjoints.

Rear Window

Sepia-blotted landscape on the bottom edge
of the drawn blind, through it the sky's
checkerboard of crossed windows against
which red bricks, frames in which people
come and go, prepare their meals, express
their personalities and emotions – two
stiff slender men stir stiffly, hover and wait,
leave the kitchen with their food and later
a stocky woman comes in and takes over
their space, works it into a broth of gesture
and steaming fragrances, while the men
where are they? In the doorway, at a
table in the next room. The slim form of
a young girl experiments on tiptoe at the oven,
carefully taking a packet from a cupboard.
Upstairs, quite methodically, she pulls her
Clothes from a wardrobe, flicks her curtain
across before becoming a sylph-shadow.
A pigeon rears up out of nowhere to perch
on your chimney in the official grey uniform
of its urban airforce squadron. Blue sky
with its puffs of lit up stationary clouds –
well there's something impervious about it,
something just uninteresting compared
to roofs and ridges, chimneys and aerials,
a plane they encroach upon in a trespass
but will never touch, just as green bark
of a tree peters out into scraggy twigs or
reaching up in witches' fingers, is frozen
in the long-creased shadows of a man
there in his dwelling-place, unspeaking.

Residues

If I cared for a person long and deep
a mind was imprinted on me;
those people are part of my weather –

each word is a ray or a shower
I feel on my skin
a little harder each time.

Memory is tangible – closer than
any song, Return to Sender,
yes, thinner than an e-mail.

When my singular world isn't there
I no longer dream of much.
I know what I have lived is lost.

Behind my eyes it seems
is just a mild vastness
and this the world plugged with tar.

When all the pearls were lead
and the oysters pried open
I muttered a singular prayer,

foiled – lost and unamused
in a glazed film, no feeling –
an absence of mystery, or pain.

The Old Unitarian Chapel, Taunton
'standing for freedom since 1720'

No entry, a Christmas tree seen through a half-obscured window.
This church welcomes all freethinking people of all religions and none
Next to the British Legion on Mary Road, in front of the park
And closed except for an hour or two every other Sunday;
A meeting on Human Rights on the sixth of January, no midweek
Guided tour. A poet and philosopher, patron saint of junkies
Preached here for a while, and a small boy accompanied his father
To hear him – here or in another nonconforming church –
The Seventh Dayers, the Baptists, Methodists and Unitarians
Clustering along this ring road thoroughfare: the town centre's
Dominated by the castle and its municipal style: castellated,
Even the Mecca's a neo-gothic bunker, wide shoulders, button-hole slits,
And Norman spires prick up across the smug market-town,
Radio-masts of an official conformity, unbroken time-lines of vicary
Gold-lettered on wooden boards, stretching back to Merrie England.
Behind this regency Unitarian Chapel there's a small cemetery,
Decayed, unreadable stones in granite, one or two surviving
Crisp as yesterday, erected here with the spanking foresight
Of somebody important who is insisting you remember his wife,
His family. Beyond lies a fresh grave, heaped with mementoes:
Two buddhas, one broken, one toppled, brass trinkets, charm bracelets,
Fluffy horses, a poem, a child's drawing, a kiss me quick hat,
A picture of the Spice Girls, grimly waterlogged, bleaching out,
A photo of the dead woman-girl at a party, prettily and blurrily lit up,
Her tinsel life extemporised by her friends in a small celebration
Of a beautiful junkie: 'Her beauty should have lasted longer'. Yes,
The Spice Girls, mossily green, floated to the bottom of the sea
To sing under a streamer-festooned tree, tricked out for a crazy wedding,
Gnomes perched on twigs, tattered fairies, wind-chimes, all the bright-eyed
Paraphernalia of post-teenage junkiedom: her life's reeling fairground
Full of toys such as we might pick up, grab at quickly in passing.
We Have to Move On – or so the plastic-covered poem says to someone.
But another hand has scored it out in ballpoint: why should we?

I Should Be So Lucky

Walking across the end of the South Acton estate
Twenty years ago, I heard that song, Kylie
Spilling out of a window, pumping
Up youth again, when I was young enough
To feel it, lucky in love, and these low
Flats and houses with mattresses
Flopping out of the first floor windows, each
Iron frame ticked out in brilliant white, neat council
Colours, and below in the longish grass
Abandoned multi-coloured trikes made of
Polyethylene, clipped together with love;
Their riders grown up now, sullen or happy
Depending on their parentage or brain chemistry.
Beautiful memories, and Kylie was there
And at home I'd put on Raw Like Sushi
And carve the top off a Fray Bentos steak and kidney
And stick it in the oven, gas mark seven,
Oblivious to irony, to everything else
That would one day come back to haunt me, who cares
A mood of quiet beauty gathering
At the dusty corners of a not-entirely-forgotten room,
Empty, it seems, in memory, and myself alone
In it, although I wasn't always, but
Definitely alone in my head, this sort of stuff
Unshareable, then as now, with anyone, at least
Anyone you happened to meet in the bars
And workplaces of Londinium. The girl of my dreams
With a real head on her shoulders, like Kylie's
Business brain, but directed to my benefit
Elusive, then, and now just an absurd series of memories.
What was I tracking on Bollo Bridge Lane
Under the railway bridge, in the shadows of the towers?
I looked up at the great tiers of their balconies
Staggering backwards into the blueness of the sky:

The eighth wonder. Like the hanging gardens of Babylon
Better, somehow, than ours, although octagonal pigeon wires
Started on the fourth floor just the same
But they already had an intercom-protected door
And kids on skateboards banged out, crashing down the ramps
Theirs to inhabit, mine to witness daily,
A warmth thing, a glass pressed to the neighbour's wall
Sounds ticking away behind the pigeon wires
And the glass started moving, spelling out words.

On Ebury Bridge Road

A streamer from off the maypole of Victoria coach station,
others to the ferry trains, to that street of bijoux shops, and
Ebury Bridge Road, the courtyards of the balconied estate
of council flats where a woman I once knew used to live,
my old girlfriend's older sister and her brood, a pair of tall
teenagers already out in the mystery world of clubs

of people you had to ignore if they didn't like you, and also
a newborn baby girl whose dirty nappy she asked me to
change, which I quickly did, as honoured as I was meant to be
carefully wiping her clean before she got me, again, to
install a flowery roller blind at her smallest window. What
use are these pretty white boys you always bring me, Lola?

Next job: to carry the tan suitcases of a Nigerian diplomat
to his black cab, brushing fufu from my fingers, and for this
she praised me earnestly, because this was how she might
obtain what she needed, a few comforts, a reprieve for her man.
I remember doing the African swoop dancing at a flat party,
her neighbour from St. Kitts: a tiny green blot on her wall.

Fela Kuti came over here on a tour sometime in the early eighties,
at a press conference cut the throat of one of his followers,
buried him there and then in a nearby London garden plot,
and the credulous press to come back next week for the resurrection
and the Metropolitan police announced solemnly: as far as
we're concerned, nobody died. This time they were right – a miracle.

He sprang from the grave, as good as new, as good as voodoo
and I often hoped our chickens would come home to roost.
Angelheart, remember how I once broke into a boarded up house for you.
We carried on for years in pain, trying to beat the odds,
reduced to a zonked silence, my pale jellyfish excuses
never good enough. Nothing to relate to but a cross-threaded screw.

Now I know you didn't love me, nor did she, your sisterhood
spoiled by unassuageable rivalry, and our love was just the same, you
always trying to override and rule me, always playing to win.
What did he have in those cases? Carrying them for a hundred yards
raised up blistered slave-welts on my curled, broken palms.
Presents for his wife, he said. Holy books, pink-flecked tombstones.

Standing in the doorway of a pub once I saw her striding past
in her full office rig, her eyes were flashing, in animated talking mode
and I stepped back into the shadows until they went on past me
out of and into my past, what an astonishing-looking woman, a false vision
you can't help but be in awe of – so it spirals on to the grave,
an endless pull of death and delusion, and you have to pull away.

My Joy, My Reason, My Dwelling

Let your arrow flow straight to my lover's heart for me
May my wounds dry up permanently or at least temporarily
May I understand the big story of ice tempests
Guide me on my way to heaven in a car of bright silver
Strengthen my understanding of where to go next
Angel of the morning, sly looks and abandonment were nearby
Where everyone sang the song somebody had written

A field is a useful article with which to tell the right time
Another way is round about the floor or wanting next door
I'd freewheeled past the library to the end of the light
On the planes the bedclothes will think of the oceans
The thoughts of the green armies of dark flying ants
I was that person so devastatingly obsessed with years

What is God? I asked the earth and it replied I am not God
And everything on earth has made the same declaration
A zoo where the animals seemed unexpectedly lethargic and dull
And the clumsiness of primitive art is the precondition of its eloquence
The brilliant minutes tremble at the ends of their branches
This town is a hole I would rather not fall to the bottom of
As I ask myself again what he would think of our escapades

Sleeping and Waking Up

Where were you when the train left the shed
As the last morning stars faded out on me
Two foxes tussled in he street, on hind legs,
Hissing and biting, black smoke puffed up
Behind the houses, a boiler screamed, blowing off steam,
Hammered sleepers, as if in a film or dream.

Where were you when my fingers tingled so
An arm dropped off to sleep before I could even
Kick away a pair of damp winding sheets; who
Was taking flash photos at the bedroom window?
A council official, a local MP or the paparazzi?
Seen through a glass wall, unbolting the taps.

Why did I rise up only to engage in talking
Negotiating an impossible peace, befriending
A strange plumber, lead him to a lower room
Where my parents sleep? Who swept it so clean?
They did, they did, or else they wouldn't stay.
Black and gold zigzags, prow of a trireme.

The room is gone, sealed doors came undone,
Foxes broke off suddenly, parted and ran along
A fork in two roads; train chugged to its buffers.
This house I lived in, it's now somebody else's
Weeds in the front yard chopped down roughly,
Tools returned to a neighbour's back garden.

Who wanted to know if I knew of an Irishman
Who would marry a Jamaican girl for money
Who listened patiently to an illegal proposition
Who feels truth keenly, doesn't know exactly.
There's a rhythm and blues tune on the radio.
Woman you need. The rack from whence I sprang.

The Fairy Castle

I spotted it peeking out from behind
A clump of bulging black binliners
Beside the blank wall of the garden shop,
Next to a door, an alley – either one
Of which could be the way it was carried down
By the parent of a child who no longer wanted it.
Too grown up? Or … what. Suspicious
Here in Harringay, the home of child murders
And complacent social services.
                                          I took it home,
I couldn't resist it. So much like – exactly like –
A larger one I hallucinated under the hall coats
With a prince and princess waltzing out of it
Before I fled past to my parents' room.
That's why I wanted it. And why I took it home.
I took the dead batteries out, wondered what
It did. Lit up? Glittered? Played a tune?
But I haven't replaced its four dead cells – yet.
Just set it up on the hall bookcase
Beside the square mirror, a place I daily pass
Where I can easily glance at it.

The rabbit was rattling around inside
As I overturned the castle and shook it.
Two loose pieces – a rabbit and a laden tea-tray,
And a slot in her little paws to hold it,
A fairytale castle with nine glittering blue minarets
And pink pennants facing every which way,
A clear plastic fountain at the top of steps
A half-open silver door where the rabbit stands
Tray in paws, to welcome visitors.
                                       None as yet.

Not much of a toy, perhaps. How could you even
Play with it? Just cheap moulded coloured tat,
A mass-produced dream within my empty pocket.
But to me, it's as if it has squeezed its passage
Out of my own head rather than Walt Disney's ample wallet.
And it sits here in all its beautiful, discarded
Fragility and hope, its pennants every which way.
The clock will strike, tea will be served,
And any furthermores – will be Welsh rarebit.

Journey to Edmonton

The buses rumble and roll,
The cars wind and honk,
The shopkeepers display their wares outside of their doors
To customers, real or imagined, sifting past or gazing out from upper decks.
So much is going on there, you see nothing, it's hidden in plain sight.
They sell strange underwear, hair extensions and, under awnings, coffee
Is hand-crafted and drunk by Turks, whose voices are warm and jagged.
High clouds pass overhead, you do not ask anyone why
This or that is happening, only continue, perhaps overhearing:

"At Wood Green, Turkish films are shown, please go here if
You wish to see girls enjoy themselves by means of excessive weeping
At the fate of a woman who has hit her head, lost her memory, so her
Devoted husband must leave her post-it notes in the kitchen
To remind her to keep looking, looking for her gone forever ability;
Returning white faced, shaken by sobs, unable to properly
Eat. At the bus station, these tears have flowed into a shallow lake,
But an astute businesswoman's dreams of expansion are unsatisfied.
These children with almond eyes, their uncles drive Porsches;
Horns outside the nicer homes of a summer evening call them out.
Although there are strong women enough to prepare Rulo Börek and
        Mercimek Çorbasi,
The boys will not stop talking to them: no wonder they are distracted.
Furthermore, these soldiers of Edmonton stand accused of fighting,
And the girls are driven onwards just like dogs and chickens.
Sometimes a Saturday morning can seem like this,
But why would a private tutor dare to complain?
Even in these indifferent times
Children from the Bosphorus will continue to keep growing.

"The government is eager for our taxes,
But how can we afford to pay?
We know now that having too many boys is bad,
While having a lot of girls is for the best;

Our girls can always be married off to the next-door neighbours,
Our sons mere foolish desirers of golden times, fast things.
Have you not seen how on the very borders of Edmonton
Ancient bleached bones of takeaways are left to be harvested?
The young people don't care for injustice, the old men weep,
And you arrive late, as if from heaven, to hear their voices laughing."

(after Tu Fu)

Looking Babies

Wish you were here with me, Leanne
& not doodling in an ingrate's kitchen,
hung over again, obsessed with Sci-Fi porn.
I'm travelling backwards, the Devon
countryside (to which I have always
been indifferent) is being left behind
again, my brother's final words
at the station: 'See you at the next funeral.'
How marvellous it would be if we
were just setting out, forward on automatic
or on this train, going somewhere fast,
our plans unfolding & for no reason
just coming out right. Why do you always
choose the wrong kind of man?
Is that me? So, you want to be
ordered around in the bedroom, hmm,
perhaps that's why you've been ordered
around in life. It's so crass, isn't it?
Forty shades of shit. Please lay off
the booze, darling! I love you to bits, you
know & I can't bear the thought
of you being hurt in any way.
Please give me the love upfront, babe
or I will be too nervous to fuck you.

Leanne, I will spank you so hard
you won't be able to sit down
for a week, your children
will just have to feed themselves,
your husband be a swine to
                      somebody else.
I enjoy the thought of him seething
at the sight of your red buttocks.
Uh oh. Don't think this one's

going to make it into *PN Review*.
Who cares anyway, sweets? No-one. No-one.
But I do, still care for you.

In the Bright Room

Everybody comes in wearing a new hat
The one they originally wore, their name
Stitched around the hatband, a special
Nickname they were once known by
The one they took on arriving
Doing some characteristic thing, not
Subject to the deformations of memory

In the bright room you make entrance
Once and forever pinned, always apart
Turning on your heel, stalk off in a long stride
A long grey skirt you used to wear back then
Or perhaps you smile shyly, and I
Pray over the open notebooks of light

These Stories

Hallucinating in a hall of mirrors
Back then I didn't know you, so glad you came
Now, to no harm, sent me this selfie
Head cocked, so many teeth, fluffy jumper.
After all, there is no eventually.

It's so hard to tell who's going to love
You the best, can only say you are lovely to me
As you always were, unrecognisably
Grown-up woman, flaky baby-girl
Your hands tied, blindfolded, trusting me

To listen to your instructions, be your
Husband's ear for music, your own
Held off desires, your girlish cruelties.
I'll always try baby, cry one more time
Against you, always undefended.

Once, when you used to go to the gym,
That boy from Kurdistan offered you gifts
To pretend to be his girlfriend, impress
His rich father. He couldn't say your right name.
Nor I, I will not betray your secrets.

She Walks in Beauty

She walks in beauty like the morning
Morbidly scratching her eczema under her mittens,
Toes frost-bitten by the stubble fields of Port Meadow
On her way to an americano (black) at Jacob's Inn
Refuelling for her morning baby-group.
What do men want from women? This
Question has been troubling her. What
Do they really want? Who knows, who knew
How to succinctly explain Black Holes
To a small boy preoccupied in heavy machinery?
Data, facts, pleased by the neat symmetry
Of reincarnation: something filling up
A void, another being popping in to inhabit
The vacuum left by some old, collapsing star.
She walks in beauty like a Duesenberg,
Her angled mirrors reflect the light of many suns,
Moons, pinched like the bottom of a waitress
By severe dieting, winter weather.

And she thinks my life is absurd!
Parents dying, bailiffs, trenchant gestures
Although none of these is without meaning
To me, just the bald order of events,
Consequences (or inconsequence, perhaps, for her)
Yet she is never far from my thoughts
Bleeping on my antique mobile
Short on instant info about ancient Greeks
Or, Christmas presents found on E-Bay.
Her distressed retro overcoat hangs from her chassis.
Woman does not live by houmous alone;
She walks in beauty, lantern of her world
And mine is far richer for knowing her.
Tell me something, tell me something nice –
It's also a bit rich from somebody who won't be told.

Vague, forgetful, an imprinted pigeon
Hopping onto the same old crumbling ledge
The way men do, and women do, too.

Regular as German clockwork racing cars
Those men she chose were granite, stolid,
Circling smoothly on a street-find Turkish rug
Until they came to rest. Perpendicular sticky magnets
For all her vertiginous filings. Why she chose them
I cannot tell. Anyway, was she so wrong?
She wonders, wandering, Joan of Arc, maybe.
Her and whose army. She walks in beauty
In a dark cloud, concealing vintage lingerie.

A Lily for My Love

Caught out there in Oxfordshire
between two panes, rebounding in starlight
angel dancing on the head of a
and too close to the ground
skittish, kittenish, lovely in your nightdress
in anything, honest to a fault
in search of wages for housework
your house in the not right order
modesty unsaved by a pin

With your allegories, your travesties
your lean recipes for happiness, your
poor study habits, your lantern eyes
inability to tell convincing lies
with your sailor tattoos, your uses
for me, your changeability, doubt
daily swings and roundabouts
routines, transparent schemes
to meet me, touch me, be touched
                                          where
A lily for my lovely Leanne
for you, Leanne, a lovely lily for my love
my love a lily for you, love my lily
Leanne, I love you, a lily for my love

Being Beauteous

You were alert to an array of possibilities
In sunlight, corsetry chafing slightly
Beneath awnings, a lawn rolling down to its river
As doubt rudely pushed its way to the front
Through the gathered throng of your admirers
That hot day in the grounds of the Karsino
Tipping its hat to the slouched roughnecks,
Village boys who'd rowed on over from Molesey
To see what the big fuss was about.
Your advent, dear. Pink sherbet on the tongue!
Highballs laced with amphetamines!
On your breast wounds sprung open, yellow and black.
Leda in a prom dress, flanked by her two little monsters
Or were you one of Loki's brood, baying forever
For the blood of a human sacrifice? Well, who knew.
The folk music of an adjacent demographic
With some overlaps, some generational modifications,
Clatters like the worn ratchet of a lock gate,
Swirls and fills the heart, rapidly
Floats us up to the lapping calm of the next level.
Tears are drawn off through an ancient sluice,
Irrigating these water meadows you'd hoped would dry up
Eventually, their gentle odour of cacaoethes
Redolent of so much scorched stubble, remembered
By a woman getting on with her dailiness.
Being beauteous, navigating along the Wey.

A return of spirit

is so often a return to whoever
we thought we were, our wants spooling
onto the floor like Leanne's jewels.
My mother, for instance,
surfaces out of her dementia
into an original fierceness,
her dissatisfaction with everything,
my dad into dogged
        acceptance & reasonable cheer.
My brother the odd creature I
tried to hold fast in the light
      of reason.
Self-acceptance & self-justification.
It's where we're all going, end up
if we are to survive at all.
                I watched your flaring form
disappear under our covers
& you surfaced from
        your assumed submissiveness
& kicked me in the head
                  a spirited mare
afraid, so afraid
& I returned to my shame you
to your stillness, trembling, tears.

Against Cutting

O do not cut yourself, my bestie
Your arm, your thigh, your wrist is my delight
When the hurt is all forgotten
The wounds will be as bright

We'll go no more a scarring
Your blood must smoothly flow
For to relieve a pressure, love
A leech will take a pint or so

O do not harm your pretty flesh
But press it close tae mine
Dinnae cut yersel, ma bonny lassie
The silver tassie's full o' wine

The blade is sharp, the wound
Is deep that festers deep within
Your breast. I may be superficial, but
Dinnae mark it on your skin

Rainham Interchange

Crossing the line to the bridge, a long low ramp
Snakes on squashed belly towards lime-green,
Brown, white, fuscia, apricot. Crayola cartons
Behind stalking pylons, a stalled wind propeller,
A few bare trees, a clear blue sky, the A13,

Pulsating abacus, shuttling artery of corpuscles.
I walk in the Hall's garden, tended, planted,
Glance at their refurbished war memorial's
Local family names, picked out afresh in multiples
Of two and three. Jay and Zak riding dirt bikes

Over the waste ground in Cherry Tree, South
Hornchurch. Jay's been kicked out of Harris Academy
Again for punching his teacher, so he asserts
In his new 'Lies' poem, whose relation to reality
Is about as indeterminate as we could manage.

They were born here. I can't get used to being
In three places at once, although I used to be
Quite good. My phone, your bleep brings you closer.
But do you guess what's on my mind, or don't you?
Nor I, anticipate your wildly swinging moods.

Sounds like they're ganging up on you. Can't you
Get your Dad onto them? What do they want?
What the fuck do they want? What deal can be struck?
You say I am wrong to say this boy is none too bright,
Or that one, Zak, is just a southpaw boxer.

Can I see you? Can I see you? Not, actually.
But you are always in one of your own places, four
Or five, offering your daily inspiration, acting

Out of gigantic moral imperatives, or respect, or
Depthless truths I just can't seem to realize.

Words are all we own, to keep our distances
Charged. Intact. The sequence is lost. It's my job
To unlock this shadow-code of greater beings,
Cast here on a screen of troubled, dancing branches
Lovely boys, whoever they or you or I might be.

Nautical Miles

Wrap your loaf around this distance
Pale pacing pylons basted with verdigris
Chatting in the restaurant nextdoor to Ukip HQ
We grind over siblings, ladle in a final
Cup of dirt, toast the past in Cobra.

Over there is Kent, the bright Medway
Hidden by Sheppey's fortress promontory;
From your daughter's upper window
Illuminated pipework furniture pumps
A somnolent river on its tideway.

On the wall, a drawing of a much
Younger Phil, white shirt, narrow shoelace tie
His fingers knotted in a cats' cradle
Looks past them all into a no space
Of art, the things he carefully made.

Grays, always too near the end of a
Journey of release, oblivion beckoning
Where a third sits down beside you
Uninvited, because he thinks you're cool
Or because he hates you for being there.

The hills have eyes, the eyes have it
& turning on a caterpillar seat to stare
Through your rearview mirror, paranoia
Is the lingua franca of the bypassed,
Orsett Road stripped memories now.

Honeysuckle has blown away forever
Like the henna in Sue's hair, angel pigment
Soon turned out to have a heart of glass

& songs we wrote in the back garden
Crying together like the bickering Everlies

Trying to reach those high notes, always
Cracking apart on the final syllable
As the final modal chord released its air
Of disconnection, severance, one last farewell,
Goodbye to the music we tried to repair.

John and Joan Elliot

John was in the coachbuilding tradition
Of burnished panels wrapped around
Wooden frames and folded, a dab hand
At the double lines with a fine brush
Encircling his dark red Austin Ruby, golden
Threads, sutures for his haemophilia.
My father and he worked together
20 years, mechanic and panel-beater, a man
Of phlegm and patience, rubbing down
Between each gossamer enamelled layer.
They droned on interminably. My ears
Stopped listening, my eyes open only to
Dusty aeroplanes hung up in the rafters
Particularly an Ajax, and sometimes
John noticed my interest and took it down
And I looked at it, not allowed to touch
Its delicate-tissued beauty,
A plane he built as a boy, his apprentice piece
Still perfect in the 1960s.
                        Joan,
A large, healthy, loud-voiced, hearty woman
Held responsibility, in one way or another
For the blown-up colour photograph
Of a giant cactus in the Arizona desert that filled
One wall of their terrace's sitting room.
This also interested me, as did the electric slide
Projector shuttling colour slides in pairs
Before my eyes, mesmeried by boredom –
landscapes, bird-life, oceans, Cacti-I-Have-Known,
On each a commentary of droning precision.
But despite their pleasantness, mild enthusiasms,
Life had proved prickly for John and Joan

Not to be grasped too firmly by its flesh
Not by somebody who could not stop bleeding.
Just thrown up on the wall, admired
And held in an uncertain amount of respect.
The cactus of death was always present
In that modest Claygate sitting room.

Her husband was sometimes hospitalised
For weeks on end: from some little nick
Inflicted at work alone in the high-ceilinged
Spraying and panel-beating workshop
Of Wellands. Chisels, screwdrivers, even rough
Carbide paper, wet-or-dry, a real life hazard
For large, gentle, ruminative John Elliot.

His son Peter grew up into another trial.
Down at the police station for threatening behaviour,
Assault, petty larceny, joyriding stolen cars.
The trouble they had with him! A tearaway,
He ran with Claygate's roughest crowd, a nasty boy
Disgusted by his parents, he threatened to hit John,
Make him bleed, and broke his mother's heart

My father and John Elliot fell out eventually
For an obscure reason that made him ashamed
And John and Joan disappeared thereafter
From our life. Until Joan phoned up to tell us
He had finally gone. His blood ran out in the end
Not long after their renegade son, Peter
Died on a crazy escapade in a stolen car
Whose marque and year I have forgotten
In the long years that have since multiplied.

For Tom and Val

I remember when I first met you
In a room above a pub, preparing
A poetry reading. I arrived early
Straight from work, to find

A neat man, almost dapper
Attired from the early seventies
Glowing yellow timberlands
A shirt of immaculate buttons

Are you Tom Raworth? Yes, that's me
Standing at a shelf perhaps
Of dark old pub wood
Drawing on a set of new white cards

A set of precise doodles
You would later pick up from a table
And hold up one by one
Oblique illustrations, I'd guessed

For a long poem shuttering through
Glowing shards of our own era
Back in the Margaret Thatcher years
Of fun and empty nostalgia

A phone call from the Midwest
Just quickly from a friend's office
A whole year's worth of CDs
Falling through my letterbox

How to say anything about it all
A blind sense of something shared
An affinity group of self-styled mind guerrillas
Had nothing much to go on

Correspondent of the almighty
They gave you a pig's heart to keep you going
You are you no longer, you
Are among our belongings

What a tragedy life becomes
When we're all jumbled together
At the bottom of the slope
Simply waiting for the next

Surgical hand to be *dealth*
Trying to give the impression of life
Much as a stone might
Pretend to be a mountain

I can no longer remember anything
An eye, a hand on the shoulder
Skating grandchildren winging
The remnants of pandemonium

This Star Makes Us Want to Lie Down

Under a spinning firework of wishbones
A wishbone is turning to a wishbone child
Nosing the ground, blood sprouting from
Her ear as the little blob-head wishbone

Springs forward on a dark blue field of sky
From her prodded spine a hip curves up
A monkey's tail waves perhaps, a small dot
Testing coal black ink on a remote corner

Two eyes, one eye, an ear, two mouths
On a sunny beach, a night scene is playing
Out for as long as we will interpret this

Through a blue window on a field of clay
This black star makes us want to lie down
Jabbing a hard rod into our curved spine

Walking After Midnight

Staring at rooms I can live in only by being outside
Where I am just another man walking in the rain
Not looking for anything, but still hoping to find it there
In the narrow alley between the ditch and the mire
Running between slats of fences and wire mesh

It is here a lean vixen has frozen in her footsteps
Her eyes glittering, guarding the direction I am taking
So that I must turn upon my heel and hurry back
Stop and turn to see her follow me once more
A dun orange freeze-frame of paused emotion

So that I have to retreat, turn right under her gaze
To walk along the road I have trodden
Oh, many times, mechanically bearing myself on
In the no-place of night time, a cornered being
Whose deepest wishes remain unsatisfied

Past help, locked in a past tense, beyond grasp
One of the old boys you might see on any street
Whether with hennaed beard or grizzled mutton chops
Left to get on with it somehow, more or less
Around the bend, or so it has been bruited

Wearing the suicide jacket, thinking unprofound
My phone has been sent to the lost property
Where I must pick it up to see who has called me
About a bill that I have left unpaid too long
Clicking off now, battery dead, a dead command

My vixen is padding on about her dastardly business
I am still wondering exactly what mine is
The unruffled past still offers me its luminous pictures
Down to the all-night garage, an empty road
Nevertheless I still look both ways before I cross

The Beacons

Here or there, it doesn't matter; anywhere at random,
Illuminating darkness, brightening up the evening,
Carried in the heart; transported everywhere inwardly
Marked our progress, showed where we had gone,
Warmed and sheltered; comforted, housed pleasantly
By marching columns, a military procession,
A chiming clock, a timepiece with bells to mark the hours
To the end of the night, the finality of a full stop.

Continuing to arise, still pushing up endlessly
Flashing over the ocean, intermittently strobing sea.
Guide the sailors home to safety, a rope to the seafarer's bed
At the helter-skelter's summit, atop its winding stair,
Bulb of topness, a bulging protuberance glowing from heaven
Tended by a daughter, the girl-child's duty of care
Lashed by waves, beaten by undulations;
A good thing for us, an object of the highest praise.

Pairs of gob-stoppers, twinned baubles of flashing light
Alternating like the terms of a predictable alercation
Penetrators of fog, shining in the cloud-shrouded dimness
Of dusk and dawn, early morning and late afternoon;
Companions of winter, a friend on the coldest days.
Riding on a uniform, astride a zebra, athwart a pelican,
Guarantor of the safety of children, temporary guardian.
A traffic regulator, calmer of too fast transportation,
Emergency brake of childhood, stiller of infant eagerness,
Commanding cars to halt, stopping automobiles.
Her name is Belisha, Belisha is what they called her.

A lost fighter in the jungle, shy entangled combatant,
A speaker of truths, utterer of the right words for justice.
Drinking her way through life, generally intoxicated
Crusader in a mini-skirt, surely an unlikely sex object.

Handlebar moustache, a bicycle of lippy growths,
Imprisoned on an island, incarcerated over there offshore.
Murdered by Stalin, rubbed out by Uncle Joe.
Dumped in the deepest ocean, buried foxtrot maritime.
Assasinated in a kitchen chair, executed tied seated.
Buried in quicklime, bitterly put under the ground.

The men who went in the aeroplanes, the lost boys in flight
The two imposters, the double agent; Mr Zig-Zag, the Criss-Cross Kid.
Uploader of secrets, disseminator of withheld information,
Campaigner for votes, agitator for more crosses for women.
A suicide at the Spanish border; no he could not get over.
A light we were following, our favourite Starbucks
A tall latte, somebody we loved, in personally-held affection.
All the nights wasted, good sleepy time frittered away
Thinking of you, bringing you to bear, holding you in mind.

In the Still of the Night

The silence of the nocturnal, the quietude of evening
Cools the earth, calming the planet's high fevers
Everything's sleeping, the world is getting its head down
A falling away of noise, discontinuation of the racket
Where insects are immobile, smaller creatures unmoving
Turning over and settling, getting comfortable to dream
The moon and the stars, our guardian celestial bodies
Sparklers in black velvet, diamonds in a soft luxury case
Raked over with a stick, agitated with spare firewood
Shucking the chaff, separating the sheep from the goats
Dripping from tubes, splishing through conduits
Filling the jugs, topping up earthenware containers
Purifying the essence, the gist of a mere complexity
Evaporating impurities, vaping off the slag
Ennobling the ear of corn, whittling at the staff of life
Wiping clean the slate, erasing those chalky residues
In the still of the night, the deep draught of absence

The heat of the day, the diurnally milder temperature
Falls from the earth, rapidly lowers as our planet
Glides on its course, flies smoothly to wherever it is going
Back to the start, maybe, recommencing at the beginning
A flawless exercise, a study in perfect execution
Rotating on its axis, turned around on its pivot of centrality
In a precise way, an exactly measurable fashion
Stately in its procession, thus pompously entrained
Where day is dawning, a light steals over the firmament
Waking up the sleepers, rousing the lightly enslumbered
To yawn and stretch for a while, to yawn and stretch
Peeping through a blind, looking past bamboo curtains
As the creaking locomotives, cold engines with elderly bones
Hoot on their horns, testing instruments of warning
Signalling movement, let us know they will be underway
Sooner rather than later; quickly, delaying no further

Down tracks of daylight, rails of natural illumination
To familiar destinations, to the places they know already
Where people await, where men and women attend us
In the warmth of the quotidian, the beat of the day

Three Dragonflies

Pallid, breastless, as if painted on the tomb
Of a Parisian pharaoh, the dragonflies hold fans
Green, blue and yellow, beads around necks,
Lifted coyly upon their long spidery fingers
In backless peacock ball gowns, unrevealing.

In the hand of each droops a cigarette holder
And in the tip a cigarette is poised languidly.
Operette-Revue, avec musique de Franz Lehár,
Adaptation de Roger Ferreol et Max Eddy
At le Bataclan, long ago, not that it matters.

Their cheeks rouged, painted lips are pursed,
Their hair bobbed, coiffed immaculately so.
Perhaps they're inviting you to a stilted party
To witness the hypnotic dance of dragonflies
For a reasonable price, a table, *tout compris*.

You will purchase a glass of greenish milk
And melt a sugar cube upon another's tongue.
Beneath a balustrade those accidental creatures
Leaned over to warn, in cries of corncrakes,
'Attendez, monsieur! The dance has begun!'

What Rough Draft

I sit here in half-amused self-contempt
Resting my bones on the dock of the bay of pigs
Nothing is further from my mind
Than improving the lot of suffering humanity
After all I'm one of them. Am I not?

Catch a crab and see where it gets you
Chew mordant fleas for the blood they contain
When this world brings you to your knees
Poleaxed between stations of the cross
On a plain of immense delirious murmurations

Imbued with the reflexive irony to mangle
Any help we might have sought or given
Nursing our grudge against the property system
Beside the still waters of Hornsey Baths
Where the legendary diving woman is capped

Traitors' gate is within us, not looming
Particularly high, and neither does the sky's grid
Unlimit my feverish self-absorption by
Denying me access to the company website
Not metonymy but deuteronomy rules us

We have to make up to our trouble and strive
Against paucity of motive. How about the
Sunbeam Jesus wanted us for? Do I have to do it for you?
O love the internet itself is thoughtless heaven
Delayer of armies, stayer of wrong executions

I left her in shadows beside the shelf of bruises
Resting her hand on the backside of a tray
A martyr to my own sort of complacent happiness
Unwrapping the last of the mordant fleas
After all, I'm one of them, I thought, in a way

Wasley's Parrot

After some time the situation became clear.
The parrot was quite likely to jump off its perch
But would soon settle down in much the same position
Its green wings ruffed up huffily around its
Scraggy neck, as if to say, "Fuck you, John."
In precisely the tone that it had been taught it
By its erstwhile master, now busy filling in coupons
In respect of some fictitious special offer,
With mixed results to judge by the opened cartons.

Green was the parrot. It had taken wing, again
Swooping, hopping, one beady eye judging
From the highest point it had discovered, near the ceiling,
On the flex hanging down from a light fitting.
Defying electrocution. Here at least the parrot was king.
Below it John Wasley. Still blinking behind his strong bifocals.
The big tache in place on his long dramatic phizog.
Once a powerfully built and talented builder.

After all, it's where any of us might finish
Some more than others as it happens, if it matters,
Nothing more to be said about it than that.
Goodbye Roy, see you soon, he sent on his wreath.
John Wasley, it was hard to credit it, the big man.
To be honest I didn't like him anymore, he
Sacred me. I preferred to remember the birds' nester.

Being Bounteous

The Gloves of the Physician, The Wisdom of the Apes, Mischievous Monkeys, An Elephant's Baggage, The Dream of the Rhinoceros, A Paddock Full of Hippos, The Boredom of the Dolphins, The Ennui of Lions, The Superciliousness of Pumas, Conviviality of the Jackasses, The Longevity of Pigs, The Patience of Donkeys, The Vigilance of the Veal, The Pluralism of the Rabbits, Why Otters Matter, The Moult of the Minks, The Prevarication of the Sloths, Addicted to Ants, The Guile of Hamsters, The Charm of the Rat, A Badger Erect, The Curiosity of the Dogs, The Happiness of the Squirrels, The Shout of the Tortoises, Two Dolorous Dingbats, A Cataract of Moles, The Conference of the Birds, The Originality of Parrots, Minor Minahs, The Anger of the Finches, Rights and Wrens, The Violence of the Hens, Investigations of an Ostrich, The Leap of the Duck, The Complacency of Whales, The Heart of the Fish, The Scurrility of Long-tailed Scampi, A Sense of Plaice, The Existence of Cod, The Greedy Goldfish, The Calm of the Wasps, The Bees' Stratagem, The Luck of the Spider, My Beautiful Bluebottle, The Glory of the Moths, The Silence of the Lamps, The Mosquito's Burden, The Delay of the Mayflies, An Enchantment of Midges, I Married a Mite, G is for Grub, The Growth Potential of Mixed Pupae, N is for Nettles, The Dock and the Bay, Grasping at Strawberries, A Providence of Oranges, The Imperious Pumpkin, Awful Apples, Illuminating the Carrot, The Hungry Yam, A Hard Nut To Crack, The Raisin's Reasons, The Shoddiness of the Grape, Tilting at Windfalls, The Edibility of Trees, The Travel Diary of an Edwardian Lady's Finger, A Fig Speaks, The Wheat Dialogues, The Usefulness of Poppies, The Rose, The Diffident Daffodil, How Green Was My Algae, The Pleas of the Plankton, A Bacterial Biography, The Microbe's Fear of the Antibiotic.

High Talk

How are you? And the maroon figure broods,
Mist rising off the mud, it's the dawn of the mud age
Of purple stripes on the blind, banjo
Accompaniment to a pork-and-beans mess.

Nothing has replaced you, murdered girl,
And the munching goat we walked past to school
Out there on the marches where time arrests
Frisking on a pathway across a field of cows.

The towers arose like seven black fingers
Out of a view I was soon to pull a curtain across
In a sensible compromise with intelligibility.
Later your brothers would say you were thran.

Your daughter is older than you, a selkie
Now with a child of her own bearing, given her by
Carmel. How could I know that name
Would always be known to me as your friend's?

People of the far parish, not difficult to judge
Once you got the trick of it. For you I was simply
Awakener and permission-giver, if you needed
Hammering I hammered you right in, for

Good, I hope, your head nodding side to side
To a tune we had promised not to remember
To forget. Your life's tumultuous adventure
Carried on for a few years, a band on the run,

From Reykjavik supermarkets to Notting Hill
I climbed up those stairs to talk, drink tea,
And after a problem-sharing session, photo albums,
You showed me your small, crumpled selkie

Fast asleep, there in her odradek carrycot.
Her mother hadn't aged a day since we first met
High above the marches, talking John Berger
And how the *Ways of Seeing* would soon alter.

Sonnet for Anne

Nothing ever so wrong as sitting in the public gallery,
The readers' gallery, with people studying football form,
Filling up Word Search books, in the Old Bailey
Waiting for your murder trial to begin, for you
To make an appearance, which you never did, did you
Only perhaps in the words of your articulate friend,
A sort of character witness against the defence
Of the man in the dock, who had slain you brutally.

Your death at another's hand was simply not to be
But an event nevertheless, the taped phonecall confession
Which fell short of reality, the dazed man who made it
Dapper in the dock holding *The Remains of the Day*
And us with our phoned-in excuses, insignificant others
Who permitted this terrible happening to happen.

To a Squirrel

That squirrel with her freeze-frame gait
Are her prime instructions loading late?
She's waiting to become unspooled
Believes she's invisible, has you fooled

The caterpillar in a packet of rocket
Lies snug inside her sealed up plastic pocket
A spider in the corner of your bed
Rehearses for her role inside your head

Her gesture wasn't learnt from us, or was it
From a wise creator must we posit
The robin inherited a drop of dew
To slake her thirst upon each instant new

The squirrel's stop-frame trick, her lifted paw
Excites a thought that we were here before
Looked out with rounded eye and paused in hope
Upon this gently situated slope

Coquette! She bounds in broken waves
This waistrel whom your generosity saves
She spurts away, but pauses in mid-flight
Lest you should have nut or two, to bite

She learnt this job, beside her mother's apron
While stirring up the soup of her creation
The spider is calm, always she is calm
She curls herself to sleep upon your palm

Chew Tar

I ring the bell, look up at the window
Bell rung, window looked up at
Adjust my tie, fiddle with the cravat
Poised at the doorstep with my sample case
Bent balloon sculptures, GCSE papers,
Encouraging smile at the ready.

I can't chat with you right now
My chew tar's here; settling on the bed
She knows the difference between mice and men
Prised up a lump of the hot bubbly stuff
Fresh from the pavement, chewed it all day.
Now she wants me to chew it for her.

Greenwich Meridian

Paco runs the Goldfish Garage, a crummy night club
Over in Greenwich, a sex haunt for Labour councillors
Who like to dress up as babies. Can you believe this?
Casey is his gofer and sidekick, a man whose father
Flushed his mum's head down their toilet, or rather
Not completely: by her neck she was still attached.

They get money from drug dealers, extorted at source.
Casey puts the frighteners on, they cough up of course
It's that or getting your head blown off. They are dross
Trading on the innocent, without a single pang of remorse.
Anything they own, they get it themselves, by violence.
Easily, due to there not being a proper police force.

Anyone who objects gets dumped in the builders' waste
Left over from constructing the new Legoland estate
And the police, they are useless, they could not give a toss
Because it's only the chavs and blacks are getting fear
Not the good people of Greenwich, the middle-classes
Who probably don't know what goes on around here.

They chase around the Cutty Sark, concreted into its bed
Exchanging wraps of sherbet and buying retro retreads
To hide the twitching in their eyes, watch the waters flow
Past the hooded barriers, around the cop-patrolled O2.
Dinky town is clogged with saddoes. Paco's robbed a few.
Now I introduce the love-rack, just like you told me to.

Ben and Sarah went out on New Year's Eve, a nice pair
Of local young lovers who'd not long before got together.
They walked home, enjoying unusually mild weather
Deciding to take a short cut though a building site
Where, as luck would have it, they accidentally witnessed
Casey cutting all the fingers off some unlucky type.

They tried to sneak on past, but Paco soon spotted them
And as the bad men came after, they ran and ran and ran
Managed to escape somehow, right back to Sarah's place
Where they ran inside and quickly phoned up the police.
By the way, my name is Ryan, it's me who is telling you this
Ridiculous nursery rhyme. It's a lesson we done in English.

My favourite film character is Freddy Kruger, from the
Friday the Thirteenth franchise. A number of insects
Keep crawling in and out of my ears. I keep them alive.
None of this is my fault, John, I can blame it on Ted Bundy.
I hope I don't end up like him, but I might do, one day.
Anyway, the police arrived in due course, I was saying,

Sarah explained what they had seen, put it quite simply,
Giving her descriptions of the men who had chased them.
The police officer said, "I know who you mean exactly.
We've been looking out for that pair, they're notorious
For cutting people up and shooting them at random;
Murderous psychopaths; you were right to report them."

He left a gun for her self-defence, returning to the station,
Bought another shooter on the way, but got a bollocking
For failing to catch up with Casey. He immediately sped
Along with his partner, Rodney, back to the Goldfish Garage.
Paco was in his office, the safe open, stashing the money.
"Hello my friends!" he cried, spreading his hands widely.

"What do you know about a strange man named Casey?"
The officer asked him, but Paco shrugged and laughed.
"He's just a guy I know, who does a little work for me;
I employ a lot of these assholes, I'm not their daddy.
Heh heh, I usually pick them up in the local dog pound.
Come back if you find out something, don't harass me."

Over at Sarah's place, Ben ate cornflakes, drinking tea,
Plotting what to do to make things turn out for the better.

He decided to go over there, mainly to check up initially
While Sarah visited Casey's mum, dying in a hospital,
Easily discovering her whereabouts on her new i-Phone 7
By means of an app she had downloaded at her leisure.

"He went funny after his brother died, he was a good son
Before that happened, tho his father was a right nasty bugger."
Sarah listened to her dying words; it was a terrible cancer
Of her throat, this poor woman could hardly speak to her.
"Thank you Mrs Casey, for the background information.
It's been lovely talking to you, understanding your situation."

Upstairs at the Goldfish, Paco and Casey were having a row
About the Feds visiting, and some spare change he owed.
Casey threatened him with a gun, snatched up a wad of cash.
Pissed out of his head per usual, Paco set fire to the stash.
Ben saw it go up from the pavement, scuttling concerned politicians
Running out in their nappies, Casey patted his burning clothes.

Ben followed him to the building site, police cars rolled in.
Sarah got there before him, hiding behind scaffolding;
Casey spotted her instantly and grabbed her by the collar
Dragging her up a crane ladder with a gun barrel held against her.
He tried to pull the cab's door open, dramatically swaying;
Sarah managed to toss down the skeng she was holding.

"Catch, Ben," she cried. Ben managed to catch the police gun
And shot it at Casey's head. He dropped her, she grabbed on,
Scrambled safely down into his arms, while Casey's blood
Pumped from his head. He teetered, lost his breath, and fell
Down to hit the ground with a thump, lying there all gone
As the Feds rolled up in their Panda car. Late as usual, John.

This is a story based on facts, facts known only to me, Ryan
Just a sixteen year old boy with no-one but his mum to rely on.
My mother is a nurse, she's a really strong, forceful person,
My sister never gets out of her pit, rarely she opens her curtains.

I took two teachers hostage, but I'd left the door wide open.
They could've walked out anytime. Basically, they're lying.

Paco and Casey are dead now, but the flavour lingers on.
Ben and Sarah got married off, beautiful children of their own.
All our girls seem to learn at school is how to work the system.
Makes you fucking sick doesn't it, romanies and gangsters,
That is what we'd like to be, it's what we know by reason.
We could complain if we wanted to, to each his own poison.

We're chavs, John. Don't ask me why it is, but we are them
Trying to cope with our issues, and make our contribution.
I have to stand up and walk around, insects are under my skin,
I wash all the time, I shave off my eyebrows to stop itching.
Not much of a life. But I hope it's changing. I'm on the spectrum.
You've got to make the best of stuff in Greenwich meridian.

Dubious Parameters

Running between high walls
Like a street thief trying to escape from the police
Is a game that's been going on it seems forever
Obviously it's not a game at all, unless a cruel sport
Designed to eliminate us left-handed people.
We have been picking up things wrong now
For far too long. Crabwise, sneaking in, sidling,
Waving a giant claw, while the smaller residual one
Flops down uselessly. I'd rather this subject wasn't mentioned again
After all, it was only a strategy I adopted briefly
To let my parents know I'd be requiring special treatment
Not a bid to have the whole wiring loom
Ripped out and turned upside-down, always sparky
As I was, if spookily homely. Better off outside.
There's only a few of us left. Right?

Much later they gave us left-handed nibs
Designed to straighten out the handwriting of the cack-handed
A curling tip slyly directing the flow backwards
Dragging black characters across the paper
So that you wouldn't splutter like a fool, an idiot;
Words were always ahead of you, unknown
Rather than appearing in languid instant retrospect.
Neither hermetic nor a hermit crab
Never learned to crook my wrist to get that crippled effect
Nor to rotate my head like the girl in *The Exorcist*
In order to observe as my stories took shape,
Implausible successions of instants, of clauses
Which is what you usually got for being pushy,
Rhyming away, as I was wont to, for the fun
That appeared, quite agreeably, out of nowhere.

I took my shape from somewhere, strumming
Right-handedly, fingering agilely with one good mitt

A tendency to repeated failed actions helped me.
My inner translation-machine bouncing its signals,
Rechannelled images as sounds, reasons as
What might have been taken for granted anyway;
Evidence flashed up quickly, an idea so easily
Picked up was just as easily put down again, forgotten,
Vividly got up as something else, your guesses
Unerringly accurate if not widely accepted,
The number-crunching abilities of Albert Einstein absent
Until a plane dropped from the sky one afternoon
When you looked up at it.
                              And yet there were always tasks
Others seemed to do more easily, pins to be pulled.
And in all modesty I have to admit I couldn't accomplish
What to others seemed completely automatic. I didn't know
Where the ball was coming from. Couldn't head it.
Expect I thought my skull was made for better things,
Although others thought it quite thick enough.
Acts of sublime genius eluded me. I flopped around
Hopped back and to the side with superb elegance
Simply afraid of my tormentors; who hated me all the more
As I put out my hand, hiding a dagger in plain sight.

Self-Portrait in a Compact

As Billie Holiday sings it, the tongue gargling
Over the bridge of sighs, not the clipped
Delivery of Dinah, dry to the point of tears, withheld anger
Or Sassy's bubbling irresponsible scat glossolalia, the
Too effortlessly ample talents of Ella
Always leave me cooler, not in need of
A julep or two. These women offered us standard fare
But they set the standard, didn't they? Bessie Smith
And her big, sliding thing: a Millicent with a trombone
Who was not about to relinquish her instrument,
She of course was great too, and that ten inch of Ida Cox
Reveals a woman who knew how to blow; but Billie
Seems to intimate she was born with these things
Around her neck, swinging pendulously to a gasped point.
Ladylike, real classy. Unwilling to dress up as a farm girl
For Teddy Wilson or nobody, betrayed, and
Mannerist to a fault, a pre-emptive strike at the ball
They hammered her around.
                         Dinah Washington
Wryly recalls September, she walks this bitter earth,
And shows Brook Benton how he *hasn't* got what it takes.
Composing herself for the microphone
Around a middle distance that's out there somewhere,
People who like their strings like low-cut ballgowns
Two rows of pearls to gawp at in the supper club
That they will never be visiting excepting in her company,
Telling them how to behave when they get there.
Somehow you know they wasted her, she herself didn't help
And yet Sarah Vaughan persuades us, and we know really it is
De-lovely to slide through intricate rhymes so naturally
Wondering where it will all end. Now it's you. So *what*?
Says Dinah. Just stay out of my spot, baby
Even if you like it, it still ain't yours to take away from me
Like the pill in a pillow, the tea in tears, wide-faced

But no longer wide-eyed. And I listen to these women
With their disposable talents, no spring fried chicken
Just a man who will squeeze a lemon till it's sweet
Because the soul is still a soul no matter how you cut it,
It fits any format precisely, replayable romantic folly
For as long as anyone bounces your ball,
The same old harbour lights calling us to order
Dancing always at the shoreline to steer us,
Announce themselves with a sort of rote indifference.
That is why scat singing is so joyous: no easel words,
Last messages, penultimate demands for rent; no
Longer needing to live in italics, but swingin' easy,
Just splashing about in the sky with a paint box;
Jackson Pollock with a bit more life training.
Better ask somebody if you don't know what you're doing.
I love the way you say *macchiato*. Thanks for the warning.

Cognitive Mapping

Nothing but the worst scenario ever comes true.
Might as well accept it, along with these multiple
Distractions; the star quality of stars
Consists in their radiance, none too grand, but all the same
Outshining local competition for administrative positions.
What were your main ideas, consciousness?
None, just the buzz of being here typing.
Everything is coincidence and charm, the rum
Happenstance of opening the book at the right page,
Shrugging into your overalls in time for the
Next trial of your inner strength; this welded wing
Will pay for my wife's breast enlargement. It's something
She and I have always dreamed of, warm pillows.

Downy substance trumps most earthly things
Although it's hard to remember well how you got here.
Simply waiting for your friends to fall over
Ready with an enamelled kidney dish to catch the oil.
I have tried to draw a picture of this many times
But most sensible readers would rather watch a horror flick
While snuggling with the fluffy ducks. The book of love.
Who wrote it? I'm wondering still as the flame
Leaps and flickers, then blues, steadily cutting
Like a hot knife through butter.
                              But all the same
The idea was good, unimpeachably consensual, simply
Blotting out people who disagreed with us.
After all, their motives were much the same as ours.
And the shapes made by the cookie cutter
Continue to be star-like, even as funding dissolves
Into promissory notes, and finally into thin air.

Margo dances before me in a strange, penumbral zone
In an industrial unit over in South Tottenham.

She runs through the forms, makes an appointment,
Turns the desk screen around so I can see the new profile
She is creating for me; copies of declarations to sign,
Forms giving automatic consent to power-sharing
Multiply at her blue-suited elbow, to smile
Wanly at the temporariness of our jobs, our tenure
And the frangible ideas that brought us hitherto
Uncharted compulsory applicants together
Under a brand new rubric, a flag of inconvenience
Self-folding, arbitrated, under scant control.

The garage is full of restless ghosts tonight,
The old Chrysler was sold off to pay a gas bill.
Although its wide running boards never completely rotted away,
They could always be repaired with pelican glue
And, repainted white, the perfect wedding car appeared
For hire on the internet. Isn't that dandy?
Elsewhere recycling took the form of daily classification
Of carburettors and sealing wax, brake fluid and string,
Distributor caps, milk cartons and ready meals
Past their sell-by date. An aeroplane is hung up
From a metal stanchion, on its wing a starry plough.
Do you think I don't wish they were all still here?

How many rivers to cross before I get over
Myself studying online maps of that warm thoroughfare,
Seven Sisters Road. A short alley where archery was practised
Furtively, taking sacs of silicon for targets.

Life in a Bowl

See how this one glimmers when you turn it
Around in the light, there's a deep blue ground
Beneath which a pair of orange poppies is trapped.
All you can do is hold it up to your cheek
As though it were an object of supreme value
Which gave off some mysterious filial heat,
Love glazed into something that caught your eye
Or mine. This whaling scene scratched on a cow bone
Too light, made of plastic in a whaling trinket factory
Broke into two neat halves by an abrupt gravity,
Its falsity revealed one day, my cheap love gift
Exposed to contempt in a way a bowl never can be.
Gathering a few petals, peaches, nothing whatever.
Brand new. Until colour fades from our eyes.

Autumn's Schedule

It's here already, piling up its tasks
Leaves clinging to the trees will first have to be torn off
Once they have kippered long enough in their cradles
Of trembling twigs, pried from the bone and then wrapped up.
Unchosen tasks completed ahead of the deadline,
Sand sloughed off the baby's bottom with a
Hose from the tap in the side wall; moth signals blown away
Their catalogued parts returned to the bowl of sun;
Work must be contemplated more seriously once again
If it ever stopped grinding its gears, bluebottle feet
Hoovered up from carpets sagging with summer's roaches,
Blood drained from weary donkeys, their ears
Laundered and replaced for hibernation;
Sandals hung up on the sandal tree to dry,
Regrets retrodden, gaps adjusted, sockets redistributed
To the correct toolboxes, people forgotten for now.

Soon everything will be tumbling out of its reticule.
The bicycle you have chosen will or will not prove serviceable;
Lady Luck will avert her gaze in feigned distress.
It will simply be a matter of expediency as to whether
They decide to follow your diagrams to the last letter;
Nimble fingers brushed aside, pavements beneath your feet,
Entraining to Vauxhall perhaps, a care home in the suburbs
Birthdays skim past, flat pebbles plunge at the limits of your wrist action
Into their ordained wave, masks donned are put aside;
Fireworks set off prematurely, sparklers sputtering,
Coups fought off or succumbed to, miscreants summarily executed
In further disquieting episodes of the Magic Roundabout.
Vaping for England, jogging to the gym, fucked.

For the moment it still feels like the end of summer.
Despite the chill those dwellings are probably of uniform
Temperature inside and out, the leaves are still leafy,

The things to do list somewhat listlessly refusing
To make as much sense as I thought it would.
Autumn's schedule is underway, starting without you,
Catching up rapidly as you try to avoid blinking.
I waited so long to be loved, not washed off prematurely.
These nibbles are nibblicious, from Land's End to Turkey
And the barely naked trees will tell it soon enough,
Broken down into delicious chunks of bite-sized goodness;
We could try that new hipster restaurant, or we could leave it
Spooling on in real time, last summer's recklessness
Proved to be about as efficacious as a rubber carving knife
On the only chicken you were able to bring to the party.
Quietly exhaling as you survey the laid out dishes.
Checking down my list. No, that's everything.

Mirrorball

I can hardly remember myself being thrown
By laser light at the walls of a dance hall
So that I split into infinitesimal particles
Accurate representations of my best self
Gathered up into one ball, projected
Everywhere at once by a giant twirling bauble
Bouncing right back all over everyone
Somebody or other stuck those mirrors on
Although I was not particularly aware of
Eyes that caught my reflection, those of others
Let us be clear, and whatever senses
They made of it. Call it a gesture if you will
Of delayed arrival, swerving away like a girl
From the revelation of her faithfulness

Always have had a sense of being prismatic
A germ in the eye of God, a faker obviously
Prefiguring images of the lake of the gone
Pissed usually on designer beers, hand-signed
By an author whose name I have forgotten
Operated like a rain-machine, its brass-themed lever
Tugging at my mind, writing it out in neat
Deliriously going through the emotions
So that the results were highly organised
But to a perverse unrecognisable agenda
Somehow I fell through into the cramped articles
Speaking in a voice unheard for years, years
Only in the public bar of the Antelope, it's
A flaking, shingled ice-cream cornucopia

But these vocabularies are well-worn
Some helper usually chips in, common currency
Long before you tried on that particular hat
Down where retro was invented, and leapt away

What did he know about it? Fussy sampler
Of bijou corporate sandwiches bought in
Ethically by the cool caterers at pop sociology inc.
No more need be said, but it always is
In gaps between mechanically thrown blades
A portrait made of matchbook covers
Depicted a daemonic monster of the age
Instead of my mum and dad and brother
Did I have to get my head half-shaved in Basildon
In search of an agglomerative synth?

Flip the switch and it starts to turn
The light guns hooded, huddled down in bunkers
Pick out airborne bombers, diffracting fiery light
Patented by now, until it is packed away
Ready for the next pseudo-festivity
The bar wiped off by a solemn barmaid
Glasses stacked in the maid-aid rack
Sad at the end of the night, this mock-sighing
Will not accomplish what it doesn't want to
Noodles flops back on an opium couch
His gone face suffused by an idiotic smile
As he remembers what? Martin Eden
Bobs to the surface, that woman in the bank
On a day off from shooting the rape scene

A few melodies recur in the aural soup
Funny how minor variation in the pentatonic is
Instantly recognisable. Hey Jew, don't slip
Say you love me when you couldn't care less
Something of a light tenor persists, right
To the final blue suede shoe or zebra cushion
Culled out of discards on the way to the chemist
Repeat prescription for infant chest relaxer
The pharmacist gives me full instructions
But this is so much heartache to someone who finds
Unpleasant things about life to be tragic

Life is shit? Forget about it in the accumulator
I don't like to interrupt his memory spiel
Where every nag clicks through to win

Meanwhile, get out and enjoy yourself
Distract the hell out of delirium, praise doubt
But regather it to a sharp point, my darling
Your three-pronged fork to stab the sleeping dead
My shards lodged in you worked right out
Through your scarless, starless skin
The yellow rose hides her thorn
Long after I tore it out and kissed it better
But let me wander away over the cliffs
Somehow bounced on, a backyard trampoline
Unmentioned, I note, our brief summertime
Of weakness, refiguration of the bloom
The mirrorball of these big ideas of ourselves
Re-embedded in a thousand reflections

I love the interest distilled in thoughts of heaven
No less than a celestial half-a-dozen react
Down to zero with a word debating
Whether to weather or soak my wethers
I find it out in prose, a lesser mouse where
Scrabble many insignificant decisions
Orders growling with their extra letter 'r'
Bang down speaker's gavel, knocking it on
The heads of the town up to the either
Muttering of gendered relationships
As if theirs weren't, code for something or other
People used to do or say things different
The past is a country where a lot of us
Drift to the mirrorball, arms outstretched

My poor friend, I remember you still
Drawing on your tight, narrow cigarette
As you surveyed the results of your marbling

I got a cardboard box immersed in
Beautiful swirls of green and black and white
Containing a pamphlet with a haiku
Opening a sly book on my near future
Your mouth twitching at the irony
A beautiful wrap. I love you gave it to me
On my fortieth birthday on the Essex bridge
And your friend ruffled my soft hair
As the cells of our cartoon multiplied
Told me I was a deeply flawed masterpiece
Making a mad control freak's exit

The algorithm of a delusion, love
Sharpens and dies like the fires in a friendship
Rivalries discarded along the road like High Line Fords
No shame, no blame. Thirty of us died
Picking out the embroidered threads on his shirt
Blindness was curable but wouldn't be
I remember a fool with a puerile sense of humour
Don't believe in magic whatever you do
It's a bartender's heaven, pictures of Diana Dors
Festooned the aisles of British Home Stores
Where she was meant to have lost her virtue
Nothing remains except her self-portraits
Several thousand of them, housed in a strong box
Guarded by fishmen in an undersea palace

It is civilisation that counts, after all
You seem to say in your much-plagiarised poem
Quoting a specious sub-aphorism without irony
Even though it was only leader writers' cant
Unlikely to be believed by anyone
Except those you were so fond of mocking
It seemed to mean raising the dead to you
Rooks ascending in a scarily vertical column
Mothers wanted to explore those rare emotions
Surrounding imagined deaths of children

There the pulse is felt and taken by us
Scribing the absolute inwardness of nothing
Pain is the grit around which a gritty pearl
Achieves its monstrous parasitic growth

Ashbery, did I think by copying sublime
Style I would become you? Not really, avoided
For twenty years, too difficult, couldn't resist
Frank O'Hara, Kenneth Koch and James Schuyler
Whose spilt milk splashed over my boots
In the summertime when you were with me
I constructed my own crystal lithium, swallowed
Jimmie Rodgers with a rough draught of
Melodies sweeter than Liebfraumilch
How can you drink that stuff? a sophisticated
Companion asked, pursing her lips in dismay
But she just didn't hear it, the racoon, the
Skunk rooting in the trash like a small dog
Goodbye big John, big everyone, gone big time

The tutors were drawn to a homophobic rant
By the beauty of its lineation, smelling salts
Dispensed by work-experience bodies
Moving to a conclusion, hard to overrule
But no, he had the friction to pay for the course
For you, the immigrant, frequently-hooded woman
What did I turn you into but poor companions
Who have the same effect as peeling onions
Dry up your damned red-rimmed eyes
And convert your self-pity into political anger
Wash it out with warm water, hold the suds
I want to be Bobbie's girl, bring shortnin' bread
Set my upper growth limit once and for all

I can only gasp at the memory of stilt-walking
Amusing muse, my dormouse to his mole
Scattered seedpods marked out the bridle path

The biker café *n'existe plus*, the jukebox
Melted down, returned to the forest floor
Needling in memory of God-knows-where
Pining for nothing, hung on the horned moon
A carbide lanthorn flickering off and out
Under *The Bell Ja*r is an ancient Mars bar
A Kit-Kat and a plain cheese sandwich
Awaiting the reinvention of pizza, drifting
Across the sky like a parachute rumour
As simple as cheese on toast, twice as tasty
Right on up to the giant paste tomato
Road Rats turned their backs if you was lucky

Illuminated manuscripts, dim bulbs
We were saving for the winter of discontent
Your friendships a stick to beat you with
Pin the tale on the donkey of instruction
Changing buses twice to end up in restraints
Alongside epic riders of dirt bikes
Zak and Jay, out there in Rainham Marshes
I shiver with them beside their libraries
Where what is given is wanted hardly
Enough rushlight to read your fortune by
Curtains twitching over the road where
A life not really lived by us poor escapees
We swung around on ropes and trees
Until the town lay done and dusted and flat

My love heart don't reply me no more
No longer fizz on the tongue of squeeze me
They batter you round the head with the
Last words, scrolling for argument
Upon the dove-grey light of the Thames estuary
Masterfully retold by a real social worker
From the republic of salvaged sureties
The Big Easy is up and running out of shrimp
The Belgian waffle bar delayed for now

She flits from table to table on her Sundays
Unable to consult her only connector
The love I bore for her wasn't too realistic
It was all I had anyway, and this is it
When her shift ends I will hear her bleep

At any streetcorner absurdity strikes you
In the face, the light without effulgence
Is a small coin harshly tossed, its distressing
Nudity elusive, and imprecations to be just
Are sterile exercises on great subjects
The important thing is to live with your ailments
Apostle of humiliated thought, still leaping
Kierkegaard's frenzied desire to be cured
Is a melody to which we must become indifferent
Camus' rhetoric a gift to the futile labourer
In the jungle of the cities, signed on
Pushing that great rock uphill as Sisyphus
Well, it gives you something to aim at, doesn't it
Any authentic creation is a gift to the future

Christ's young face, wide eyes and mullet
Well-groomed, parted beard. Cool belied by
A long hand laid upon his own breast
As he greets Roman soldiers in Gethsemene
Was it his birth unleashed nightmares?
No, he was the blessed saviour of mankind
One way of looking at it, probably
William Blake's restful tempura gives us
An English Jesus, option of thinking what we like
There's confidence sure, an inner certainty
But no rays shooting out of his head
The bug-eyes have it, his plucked eyebrows
No doubt once excited a comment or two
He withdraws, unsure what will happen

And yes, there's nothing I want to leave
Behind but to redraw it into a greater pattern
The path set out upon and trodden
Slices of salami you carved off to the end
Here it is again, bean news for nobodaddy
As the earth dies screaming for mercy cruel
Masters claim they would have given us
If only we'd known how to ask for it properly
Cararacts a defence against the glare of screens
Dogs of investigation, eagerly desiring
Lolling at last we stand up for you
Take your gifts and turn them over curiously
Perfect, what we had wished for all along
Jesu offereth his long-fingered blessing

A victim of the God delusion, ringing
In my ears microsuction has not completely
Excavated: a steady modulating strum
Choirs of angels discerned, sometimes a
Series of instructions, write this deadly sonnet
You don't think you'll get away with it
Do you? Should we recognise divine helpers
By the severe bollocking they give us?
There is a real sense in which thought is money
I can't help thinking these prolific types
Guided by the new spirit are taking dictation
Whereas it might be the lure of an advance
High motives reveal themselves as power sins
A sort of linked-in network of spirituality

Somebody needed to climb up on that cross
And taste the vinegar, but there seems
Some confusion about who is doing the suffering
Exemplar of victory in defeat, that being
Whether it's the noble mind of Christ
Pales out our measly quotient of woe
Or did he do our suffering for us? Surely no

He offers to exalt us, Deckard grasps
The handles of the empathy machine
When really what is wanted is an answering
Of grief; but it seems those who hear it
Are lost to us also, wanderers on the shoreline
Collecting those fossils, ammonite whirligigs
Looking up suddenly for no reason

A year's come round, I scarcely know
Myself sometimes, grey ghost scary to teenagers
No, not frightening, just an illegal alien
From the distant past, a wild garden of
Errors untamped down, untrimmed
Relieved to be released from supervision
I like people who pelt cars with stolen eggs
Stop tube trains for a laugh, irritating
Everyone but talking their way out of harm
The feeling's not mutual, not really
I want to say something to them, but what?
Imprecate, apologise, dodge questions
Saluter of greatness, scourge of the fallen
My enemies died, but not all of them

And may this be placed upon your diadem
Dim enough beside the gaudier jewels
Although not particularly trying to stand out
As palinode or palisade, stepping to
Retreating waves, letters posted in quicksand
Spent pens planted and covered in polyps
Leaching out into squid ink tides
Herons peck and the gulls wheel, plummet
To investigate a squirming thought or
Palings to be perched on, predicates
Half-remembered from goon show scripts
At the back of my brain always the city
Another box of fudge altogether, isn't it?
As musos pack up their bows and fiddles

Blues guitarists are hammering on
In Sidmouth, their once disobedient digits
Long ago trained to boogie for shoppers
Knots of them on the pavement
Audiences for the oomph, the didgeridoo
Loping circulating bass routines easily
Outclassing these obese morris dancers
Who're carrying a virgin with antlers on her head
Arousing our indifference in all its
Crummy sifting of nothingness
Until the bluesmen have almost forgotten
The origin of their tunes in progressions
Across silver strings, the fretboard
Burnt fingers of old men remembering

The tidal crash of freezing waves betrays
Lack of a filament to warm it through
No need to splash around, just look at them
Who turned off the electric, not I
Nor any of my closest friends, my friends
Who feel around their clever lives by touch
Geoff, for one, no Bonio please, no doubt
How long since we both trailed along along
Left nothing but a faint pattering of rain
A ball of wax, the whole nine yards of
String to lace up my wind-sole shoes
Always a tree-bound spirit, waving high up
At an elevation I was scared to share in
Climbed up anyway to lie on a bough

Such copycats, aren't we, dazzled ourselves
Yawning in the morning of our lives
Our loves mere bagatelles, our hopes were
Something more than we deserved richly
Bowing to get the congressional medal
Such a disappointment at the finishing end
Fuck em all, and rage against the dying light

Beside the green bay of cauldron smoke
Our prayers and meditations offered up
With whatever sincerity we could muster
Those tricks of the light didn't matter much
Except to those who mastered them
Hung up on the washing line, the fake fakir
Insisted that the cards must be redrawn

I can't believe it either, stepping forth
From the shadows my invisible helpers, you
Have actually been there all along
Charging the night air with your presence
Almost ghosts, you kept jerking the line
Me awake, providing all those little windows
Where I see myself somewhere in the past
Rubbing ointment in a sore place, watching
As a messy infection retreats, gives up
Hope reappearing to offer its dubious balm
Enough vista of a hill climb no more than
An obvious bus turn beside some bogus
Landmark that will later define the area
Never resting assured, fitfully going on

Banking receipts, hassling through turnstiles
Turning each obstacle into a gate to
Somewhere we didn't know we wanted to go
But go we did, luckily forgetting every last
Mile of the journey. Years and years and years
What can you say? Breathed in and out
Used the cashpoints drawn on the same
Savings account I opened after my credit
Rating disappeared abruptly. Window
Shopping lunch breaks in New Bond Street
Unpriced items sand between your toes
Who bought those hideous silver linings?
In Berkeley Square the black cabs circulating
Dung beetles rolling the rich around

How tedious their itineraries, destinations
Working your way up to that for what?
The corniest songs always the most chewy
The moth imitated a twig of silver birch
Nature's absolute mimicry of forms
Mind-boggling algorithms of deselection
The rays of the messiah we marketed
To turn our hands in on the beaten dancefloor
Preferred the riderless horses I witnessed
Galloping along fiercely between
Dark railings of headlight mansions
Going somewhere, going nowhere perhaps
Fuming and foaming, blindly galloping
My helpers! Shake out your glorious manes!

www.ingramcontent.com/pod-product-compliance
Lightning Source LLC
Chambersburg PA
CBHW031207160426
43193CB00008B/543